# Acrylic Painting

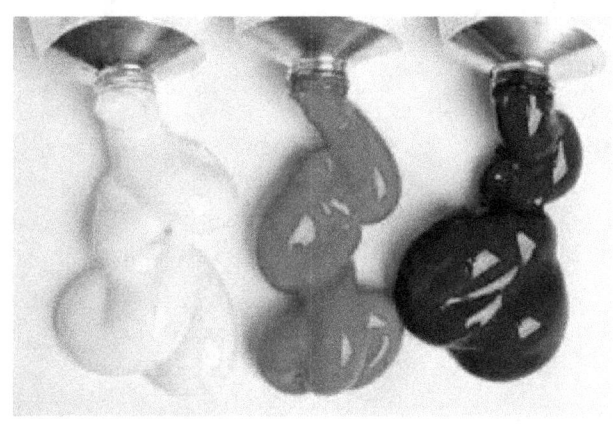

## *Beginner's Guide To Everything You Need To Know About Acrylic Painting*

# Table Of Contents

# Introduction

A rt has evolved and developed over the years. It now comes in many forms through different techniques, and with the use of different materials and resources. However, despite these variations, the purpose of art has remained the same. It is to relay to its audience a meaningful message through a creative manner.

Painting is one of the different ways of art expression. Through the use of paint, brushes, and other materials, artists are able to convey their emotions and messages in the most passionate way possible. Painting can both be a profession or a hobby. A number of people devote most of their time completing their masterpieces, while others enjoy the art of painting in their leisure time. Regardless of how people express their love for painting, every painter, whether professional or aspiring, agree that it is a fulfilling activity.

To aspiring and future artists, I want to thank you and congratulate you for downloading the book, *"Acrylic Painting: Beginner's Guide To Everything You Need To Know About Acrylic Painting."* This is written especially for young artists who want to see themselves as successful painters one day. This is made for those who aspire for their works to be seen by the world. Through the lessons in this book, they can let the whole world know how effective painting is as a way of communicating and bridging the gaps across different nations and cultures.

This book contains proven steps and strategies on how to do the basics of acrylic painting and to help beginners on their journey to a fun and artistic acrylic life. It also contains basic information about acrylic paints to help its readers determine what kind of acrylics to use.

Help us share our love for painting to other people by encouraging them to get started with their artworks. After all, painting does not require professional drawing and artistic skills; it only needs passionate and creative hands. Thanks again for downloading this book, I hope you enjoy it!

# Brief History of Acrylic Painting

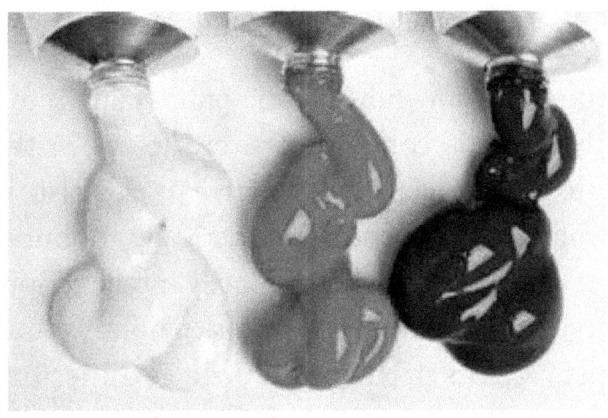

Before getting into the basics of acrylic painting and the different kinds of acrylic paints, it is important to know the history of acrylic painting. Having a background of how acrylic paints were discovered will be helpful in knowing their compositions and how they will affect the quality of your work.

This chapter introduces the brief history of acrylic painting. It aims to give the readers an idea of how acrylic painting came into being, and how it has developed as one of the most creative and effective medium of art expression.

Acrylic painting is a modern medium for painting, as compared to the commonly used oil and watercolor. The history of acrylic painting can be traced back to the past century – a proof that it has just emerged recently. The use of acrylic paint in painting is known for its unique features, such as versatility, durability, and immediacy. What attracted painters to use acrylic paint are its bright colors, as well as its ability to be applied on different surfaces and be mixed with other media.

It is important to know how acrylic paint came into existence. It is said that acrylic compounds were found in the mid-19th century. Otto Rohm, who was a German chemist, introduced how these materials can be used practically. Rohm's discovery and study of acrylic resins was primarily intended for industrial use. The first acrylic emulsion artists' paints were the Politec Acrylic Artists' Colors produced by Jose L. Gutierrez in Mexico and Permanent Pigments Co. of Cincinnati. The first water based acrylic paint available commercially was placed on the market in 1955. It was during 1963 when an artist's acrylic color in Europe was introduced. Rowney manufactured it under the brand name Cryla.

As pop culture, photorealism, abstract expressionism, and pop art evolve and develop, acrylics become in demand for artists. They use acrylic paints in expressing these art forms. Many artists in the later 20th century appreciated the use of acrylic painting in art expression because of its features distinct from oil and watercolor painting. Its flexibility and versatility unleashed creative possibilities in painters and art enthusiasts alike.

Eventually, acrylic painting evolved and new techniques were developed, as will be introduced to you in the chapters to follow.

Acrylic painting is a form of painting that was developed in the late 1940s due to the fact that this paint was not developed until that time. Because of this, there is not much history to this form of painting since it is so new compared to some of the other methods of painting such as oil and watercolor. The polymer-based acrylics first entered the market as a type of house paint, but it had so many benefits that it was soon brought to the attention of various painters. It did not take long for acrylic painting to be used and by the 1950s many artists had begun to use this type of paint in order to avoid the hassles with a long drying time like what was found in oil paint. These artists also found that the synthetic paint ended up being very versatile and it would give them a lot of potential when it came to the work that they were doing. As time went on, many manufacturers began to improve their methods of formulating these paints so that the paint would have a richer pigment. Although it has proven that it can be very versatile for artists, it is still pretty new and so there is not a lot that has been done with it yet.

For quite a few contemporary artists, this type of paint would become the perfect vehicle that they could use in order to drive their crafts. With the wide range of possibilities that these paints could offer, artists were able to use them for anything from layering like in oil paint or using it to get the effects of watercolor. In addition, these paints could also be mixed into other types of media works, such as a collage, and still look great, which allowed many artists more chance to experiment with what they were doing and create something that was completely new. There are a few limitations that come with this kind of paint though. One of these is that it is going to dry quickly so it is almost impossible to do blending or other wet on wet techniques. This can create a boundary for some artists, although some really like the fact that these paints are able to dry so quickly. Still, there are a lot of artists who love to work with this kind of medium to get something that is completely new.

There are many different artists who have used this kind of painting in order to make their creations. For examples, Andy Warhol was known to explore the different affects that are found with acrylics. In his "Campbell Soup Can" which became really well-known, he used acrylic in order to demonstrate the bold and sharp clarity that is possible with these paints while on the other hand his "Little Electric Chair (Orange)" shows how grim and dark these same kinds of paints are able to be. This is just one of the artists that is known to use this kind of paint in their work. Another example is David Hockney's "Three Chairs with a Section of a Picasso Mural." In this painting the acrylics are used in order to provide a type of softness to this watercolor. Another painting by the same artist "Rocky Mountains and Tired Indians" uses the same paints in order to create a sharpness that is similar to what can be found with oil paints. These artists used these paints in order to show all the different things that could be done with them. They are not to be viewed in the terms that are given to the other media because acrylic is something that is all its own with endless possibilities.

Even with such a short history at play, acrylics have been able to captivate the human mind and get the attention of many different artists. There are many modern paintings that have used this form of painting in order to make something that is truly unique and there is no doubt that it will be used over and over again.

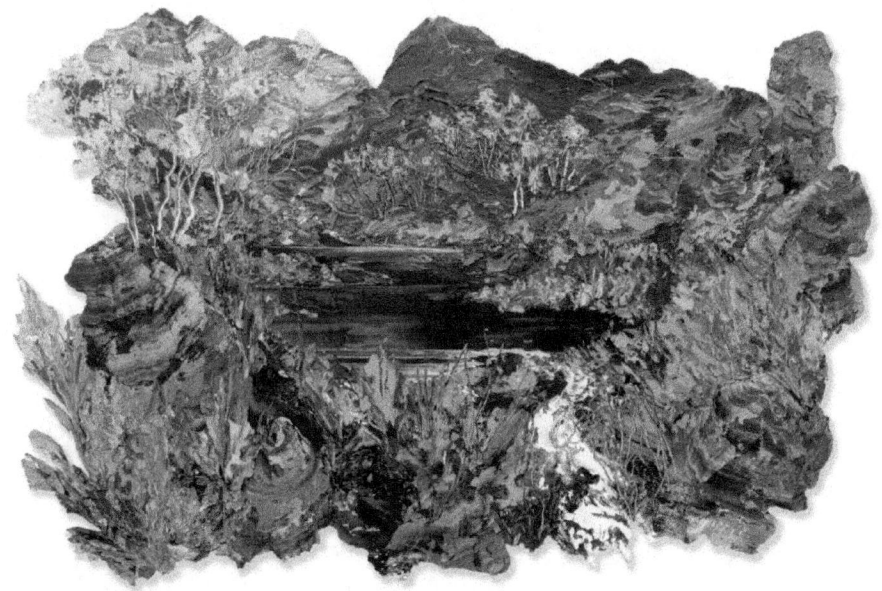

James Hawkins – Acrylic on carbon fiber

# Things to Know About Acrylic Painting

**B**efore you get started with using acrylic painting for your own uses, you might want to make sure that you understand some of the more important aspects of the artwork. This type of painting is one that is really rewarding and can be a great pastime for those artists who like to use a type of paint that is both versatile as well as challenging. Artists who use this kind of paint are going to be able to change the properties of their acrylic paint, or leave it the same, in order to get the exact look that they are going for. The challenges that come with this kind of painting can often be overcome simply by knowing that they are going to happen in advance; this can help you to make a plan for when it occurs so that the painting can continue to go smoothly.

There are a few things that you should keep in mind when you are doing acrylic painting. To start with is that this kind of paint is going to dry very quickly. You are not going to get much time once you make a paint mark in order to fix it, which can be nice if you want to get the painting done quickly but can cause some issues if you place too much on your palette and are not able to use it all up. Wasting the paint can get really expensive so it is a good idea to only squeeze out a little bit of the paint at a time and make sure that you are using it right away or finding a way that you will be able to keep it moist. You also need to be careful because most acrylic paints are going to be really difficult to remove from any surface once they have had the chance to dry. If you make a very large mistake, it is possible to use a solvent to help out, but this is not an option if you make a tiny mistake. These solvents are going to remove all of the stuff on the page down to the canvas meaning that you will probably lose all the work. So work quickly, be away that the drying is going to be fast, and only work on one part at a time for the best results.

The fact that this paint is really fast drying means that it is going to be difficult in order to blend things on the canvas after just a few minutes or a little bit longer. This means that you are not going to be able to wait twenty minutes or longer and then do the blending that you want; you are going to have to do it all at once in order to get the desired results. To get through this challenge, you will need to make sure that you are painting small parts of the canvas as much as you possibly can before going on to the next part. This also means that you must have some idea of the details that you plan to add to the painting so that you know which ones are going to require blending before you get started so that you are able to incorporate them as you go.

If you are trying to get the best results with this kind of painting, it is good to take the time to prepare your canvas. This can be done with some artist grade gesso. To get the canvas all prepared, you should smooth the gesso out onto the canvas and then place the canvas in an area where it is going to have plenty of time to dry without getting hit. Allow the canvas to dry completely before you get started with the painting. This is not a step that is completely necessary, but it will be a nice thing to do if you want the paints to mind to the canvas in a more secure way. It is also important to note that gesso is available in a lot of different colors so if you would like to try something different out on your painting, it might be a good idea to choose the color of the gesso to work with your painting.

If you would like to change up the colors that you are getting with the acrylic paints, there are some ways that you will be able to do this. Often additives can be used in order to make the paints either thicker or thinner. The additive is considered to be one of the best tools that an artist can use when they are doing this kind of painting. This is because they are able to change how thick the paint in, which is in turn going to make an amazing product to enjoy. Not only that, but they are going to be able to change the type of finish, the level of transparency in the painting, as well as the time that it takes to dry. If you would rather have the paint be a little thinner rather than thick, it is possible to do this as well with a little bit of water. It is best to use only a little bit of water on your paints; if you end up using more than 30 percent of water to mix into the paint, the paint is going to start to break down its properties and it will end up being useless.

Another thing that you should remember to do often is to blot out your paintbrush when you are doing this kind of painting. When you are using the thick paint, the paint is more likely to dry up really quickly and it will then form into thick globs all over your paint brush. Using this blotting technique will help to get these globs off the paintbrush so that they do not stick and you are able to continue on with the process. If you are using the thinner paints, you might find that the extra droplets that are on your paintbrush are going to run off and into your art, making the picture not turn out the way that you would like it to.

For those who like to do something that is considered a mixed media artwork, acrylic paint is the way that you should go because it is able to lend itself easily to this form of work. These types of paints have proven to be almost impossible to get off after they have had time to dry. This means that the artist is able to use charcoal, pen, chalk, and oil paints as well as other types of artistic mediums on the painting without having to worry about ruining the work that they did already with the acrylic paints. This allows the artist to create something that is truly amazing that is not possible with some of the other forms of paints.

Cleaning up after using this kind of paint is really important, but it is a process that is not going to be too difficult. This is because this type of paint is considered to be water soluble; this means that you will just need some water and a few towels in order to get all of the cleanup that you have done. Make sure to place your paint brushes into water and rinse them off before drying all of the way through. You should make sure to wipe off your work surfaces right after you are done with any spills. If you do not, there is little chance that it is going to come off later since the paint will dry and it often will not get better.

# Reasons to Choose Acrylic Painting

There are many different types of paints that you would be able to us if you are looking to get started with some form of painting. Each of the different paints are going to give you some freedom and choices in how the finished project is going to look. Some of the options might include water colors, oils, regular paints, and even charcoal paints. Some of these are going to show up as really bright and deep colors and others are going to be more light and airy. With all of these options, you might be wondering why you should choose to go with acrylic paints rather than some of the other options that are available.

Acrylic paints are usually made from the pigment which has been suspended in an emulsion for acrylic polymer. This is basically a mixture of two different substances that are not able to blend together. The result ends up being the great vibrant colors that you are able to see in the acrylic paints. These kind of paints were not available commercially until about the 1950s and then they were used mostly as a companion to the oil paintings because they worked well together. Many different artists like to use acrylics because they are easy and quick to dry, which is completely unlike what happens in oil paints, and there are so many different things that you are able to do with them.

Another of the benefits that you are able to do with these kinds of paints is that you can make them into something different than what they were to start with. You are not stuck with the way that the paints are originally which can allow you to have a lot of options when you are trying to do a painting. For example, one thing that you can do with these paints is dilute them down using some water. When these paints have been diluted, you will end up with a finished product that looks a lot like a watercolor. In fact, there are times when people are trying to make a watercolor like picture, they will use the acrylic paints because the color is going to end up drying closer to the color that they are looking for; usually this is a color that is a little bit darker than what occurred when you first applied it to the page. Watercolors are the ones that are going to end up drying out lighter than when you put them on and it is difficult to predict how light they are going to turn out. So if you want a watercolor like picture that is a darker color or that you are able to control a little bit more than with watercolors, using acrylic paints is the right way to go.

Even though you are able to use water in order to dilute the paints to make them into lighter colors, once the paint has dried, it can be really resistant to any water that comes near it. This is a great feature because you know that once you are done with the painting and have it exactly the way that you would like it is going to stay that way for all time. You are not going to have to worry about the painting getting messed up and the final piece is going to stay just the way that you want for a long time to come.

It is often that you will be able to use these kinds of paints instead of using oil paints because it is much easier to use and the colors are going to dry faster than what you will get with oils. In fact, most of the painting is usually able to dry within an hour or so and sometimes if it is done in the right way it is going to dry in a lot less time than that. They amount of time that it is going to take for these paints to dry is going to depend on a variety of things including what type of brand you are using, if you have changed the tint at all, and how thickly you are applying the paint. The fact that there are so many other uses that you can get out of acrylic paints compared to the oil paints or even watercolors makes it the ideal choice that you should go for in order to get the perfect picture each time.

If you feel like the acrylic paint is drying up too quickly and you are not able to get all of the blending techniques and other little tricks in that you would like, there is an answer to help with that. It is possible to lengthen the time that the acrylic paint takes to dry simply by mixing in a type of retarder or extender. You will be able to purchase these products at most of the large art stores or companies. Extending this drying time of these kinds of paints are going to make it much easier to blend the colors together while you are working on the art piece. Those who are using the acrylics in order to paint model figures find that using the retarders and extenders can make the job a lot easier as do those artists who are using these types of paints because they prefer them over the other options but they feel that the drying period is just not long enough for their piece.

In addition, the use of acrylic paints is thought to make the project last for a lot longer time period than what can occur with some of the other types of paints. For example, paintings that are done with oil paints often have a tendency to become yellow as they begin to oxidize and age over time. On the other hand, acrylics have so far shown no signs of cracking, yellowing, and changing in the last 50 years since they were first invented. This means that the paints are much more durable than other options and you are going to be able to get a marvelous piece that will last for many years to come.

Here are some more of the advantages, as well as some of the disadvantages that you may come across when you are dealing with acrylic paints in your new paintings.

**Toxicity Levels**

Advantages: to start with is going to be the advantages. In terms of the toxicity levels, these types of paints are considered to be water based. This means that they are able to be thinned just using water and that no toxic spirits or other things are required to make them into a thinner color. In addition, any of the wet paint that you are using will be able to be cleaned of the brushes as well as other materials simply by using water and soap. There are no issues with using toxic materials with the paints or even when you are cleaning things up.

Disadvantages: depending on the brand that you are using, there are some of these kinds of paints that may contain toxins with the pigments, similar to what can be found in some of the oil paints that you might be using. Using a retarder or an extender in order to slow down the drying time, remember that the drying time on these kinds of paints is really short, is going to introduce even more toxins into your paint so it is important to be careful when you use these paints and when you use some more additions into them.

## Drying Times

Advantages: one of the benefits of using these kinds of paints is that they get to dry really quickly. You will not have to wait for hours or even days in order to get the painting to be dry enough to use. In most cases, you will be able to get the paints to dry in an hour or so. For the traditional forms of the acrylic paints that do not have any extenders in them are going to dry really quickly. This means that you are not going to have to wait between the different painting sessions in order to dry in order to layer them. You can do it all in one sitting or within a day if you would like. If you are going to need to ship the painting, it is going to be dry enough that you can ship it in a day or so.

Disadvantage: because these paints are able to dry really quickly it can sometimes be difficult to get any blending done in order to create a kind of wet in wet technique like what can be done and which is popular with many oil paints. This means that you are often going to get a look that is much harsher than what is usually find in the oil paintings. Another disadvantage is that you have to worry about acrylic paint drying really quickly on top of the palette. While it is possible to purchase a special palette that is designed to keep these kinds of paints wet and workable for a longer period of time when they are outside the tube so that helps. But if you are a slower painter it can sometimes be a problem using the paints quickly enough before they begin to dry up.

## Reactivation

Advantage: there are other types of water based paints, such as water colors, that are difficult to color over if it is needed. Even though acrylic paints are ones that are considered water based, they are easy to layer on top. This is because the paint is going to dry and stay on the canvas or other support to stay for good. This means that it is easy to paint new layers on the ones that are already on the canvas.

Disadvantages: one of the most difficult things to deal with in concerns to this kind of paint is that once you have let it dry, it is impossible to get it removed or altered in any way. This means that you are stuck with the lines or designs that you have created even if you do not like them. This is why it is a good idea to make a drawing or have a great idea of what you would like to paint ahead of time because you are not going to be able to change it later.

## Durability

Advantages: these kinds of paints are very durable and provide the painter with a lot more flexibility compared to using oil paints like in traditional paintings. There is no need to go over and follow some of the traditional rules such as the fat over lean when you are using acrylics because you do not have to worry about them cracking in the end. Once you put the acrylic on the page, it is going to dry really quickly and you are not going to have to worry about it breaking, cracking, or coming off at all.

Disadvantages: the acrylic paints are fairly new which means that they have not had the time to hold up over a longer period. Yes they have done an amazing job over the last 50 years since they were created, but it is still uncertain how they are going to do over a long period of time or for hundreds of years. It is still going to be some time before they are able to prove this or not. On the other hand, oil paints might not seem as durable, but they have been around for hundreds of years and even though they are starting to crack and peel, many of these paintings are still around. Certainly, the different types of acrylic paints appear to last a lot longer and be more durable at the current time compared to oil paints, but it is important to remember that these kinds of paints have not made it through enough time to see how they are going to fair.

## New vs. Old Acrylics

There are also some advantages and disadvantages that occur when you compare the traditional acrylics, like those that were discussed above, with the new acrylics that are being produced. These new versions are being produced in order to make it easier to paint with acrylics so that you are able to get the best pictures. This next section is going to spend some time talking about the differences between these types of acrylics.

## Toxicity Levels

There is no proof that there are any differences between the traditional forms and the newer forms of acrylic paints in terms of the toxicity levels that they have. The only difference to consider is that the newer versions have been set up to have a slower drying time which means that you will not need to use the extenders or retarders. For the most part, these were the main source of toxins in the traditional form of these types of paints so if you are able to reduce the use of these extenders or retardants, you are able to lower the amount of toxins. But between the regular form of each paints, they are the same.

## Drying Time

Advantages: the newer versions of these paints have a longer time for drying so that you are able to leave out the paint on a palette that is sealed and it is still going to be usable for a few days. Also, you are still able to do the wet in wet techniques that are found in the oil paints, but you will not need to use a retarder to do them. This all means that you are going to be able to paint without worrying as much about the drying times when you are using these kinds of paints. In addition, the use of blending can come into play with these newer paints and the whole process can become easier.

Disadvantages: These paints might take longer to dry, but that means you are going to have to take more time to let them dry before you can add on more colors or before you can do something else that you would like with the painting. For those artists who like the fact that these paints allow their paintings to dry quickly, it can be difficult to use these kinds of paints.

## Reactivation

Advantage: These newer paints are able to reactive compared to the other traditional forms that are not going to be able to be workable again when applied with water. This means that with these newer paints, you are going to be able to apply water to the paint that feels dry to the touch and you will be able to reactivate it, lift it off, and work it again. Over time, this ability is going to be lost in order to help preserve the painting, but in the beginning you are going to be able to do a lot with it. This opens up some choices and freedom to you when you are working with these kinds of paintings. You will be able to fix up your mistakes, move things around, and even clean up off of other materials if you end up spilling some.

Disadvantages: this new feature can sometimes cause issues when you paint the new wet acrylics on top of some of the old ones. Often you are going to have to deal with some color bleed.

These are just some of the benefits that you are going to be able to get when you choose to use acrylic paints for your next project. As you can see, there are quite a few of them that can make your life easier and provide you with some amazing pictures as long as you are prepared and you know what to expect.

# How to Choose Acrylic Paint

crylic painting is something that has been around for a long time and allows you a lot of freedom in what you would like your painting to end up with. The best part about acrylic painting is that there is wonderful quality found in the paints as well as a great vibrancy that cannot be found with some of the other choices in paints that are out here. This means that you will be able to create a great and unique project without having to spend as much of your own time or money compared to the other methods that are out there. There are many people who will pick up this kind of painting in order to count it as a fulfilling hobby and it can even be a good starting point if you are not sure if painting is the right choice for you.

If you are interested in getting started with painting with acrylics, this chapter is going to help you out. You will learn how to paint with this wonderful medium and make some of the best pictures possible.

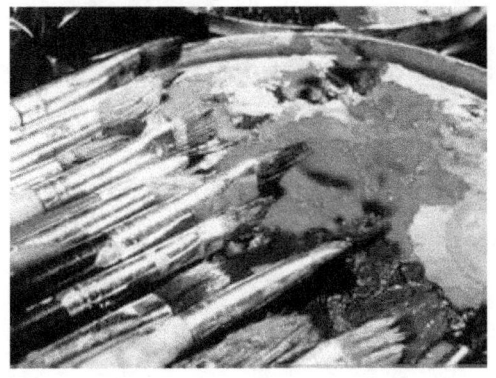

### Choose the Paint

The first thing that you need to do in order to get started with this form of painting is to choose them out. There are at least a dozen brands of acrylic paints and you will also be able to choose the container that the paint comes in, whether you are choosing jars or tubes. In most cases, you will be fine purchasing the brand and type that is cheaper since they are pretty much the same; in the case of your acrylic painting, it is best to choose a pricier and better brand in order to get the best results. The cheaper brands of acrylic paints are often less pigmented so you are not going to be able to have the deep and dark colors that you are looking for when you go with acrylic paints. If you do go with the cheaper brands, you are going to have to do at least two or three coats in order to get a dark color that comes with just a single coat of the more expensive brands, which means that you are going to end up paying more in the long run this way. Go with the more expensive brand in order to have the best results.

Some things that you should keep in mind when you are purchasing your acrylic paints is that you should buy the most basic of colors. This would include colors such as yellow ochre, alizarin crimson, ultramarine blue, mars black, and titanium white. If you do not have a lot of money to spend on the acrylic paints when you get started, it can be helpful to just purchase these important colors since you will be able to combine these ones together in order to make some of the other colors that you need.

Another thing to keep in mind is that you should pick out the tubes when you first start out. This is because you will be able to purchase the tubes in smaller quantities. This can make it easier to just try it out without spending a lot of money if you are not sure if all of this is going to stick or not. You can experiment with all of this before you waste a lot of money with the more expensive tubes of paint. The best part is that there is not any difference between the quality that is in the jar of acrylic paint and the tube that you are using.

**Select paintbrushes**

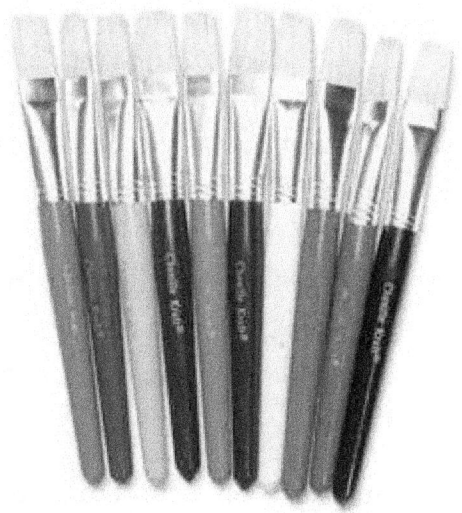

After you have chosen the paints that you would like to use, you need to pick out the paintbrushes that you like. Most people do not realize it, but there are a lot of different kinds of paintbrushes that you will be able to choose from. For the most part, there are two factors that will help to categorize the paintbrushes that you can choose from. These two factors include the material that the bristles are made of and the shape that the tip of the brush comes in. To start with is the different types of brush tips including filbert, rounded, and flat. There are also a lot of different materials that can be used to make the paintbrush bristles even though the most common include boar hair and synthetic. While all of the different brushes will do a great job for helping you paint, you will be able to do different things with your paintings depending on the brush that you choose to use. For the most part, beginners are going to choose synthetic brushes that have an assortment of tip points.

When you are determining which paintbrush you would like to use, you should go to an art supply store and take some time looking over the brushes that they have. You could gain a feel for the brushes for a good idea of the kind that you think would work best. Most beginners are fond of using the synthetic brushes because they are a lot softer, easier to use, and easier to clean out when you are done compared to brushes that have real fur.

With your paintbrush, it is often a good idea to not spend a ton of money if you are just starting out. It is important to have good paint brushes to get started out, the paint is going to be something that is much more important for the whole process. Start out with some cheaper paint brushes and try out the process for a little while. If you decide that you want to keep going with it for the long term you can always go back and get more paint brushes that are nicer.

## Find Color Palette

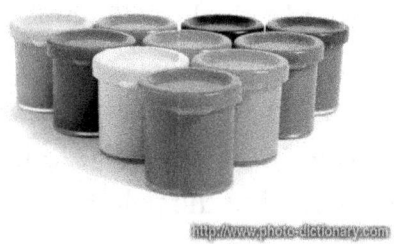

http://www.photo-dictionary.com

While you are at the paint store, it is important that you take the time to find a palette that you can use to hold and mix the paints that you are using. It is also a good idea to find one that you will be able to keep the paint on for storage between your painting sessions. If you need to save money or just want to try out the whole process for the first time, a plastic plate or paper will work to start with. Any of your surfaces that are clean, flat, and wide will be able to work as a palette. It is best to choose a palette that is able to stay a little bit wet since you will have to worry about the pains drying out really quickly and you will need to keep them wet. There are also some color palettes that will incorporate some stay wet paper and a wet sponge that helps you to keep your paints moist and workable for some time if you want to store the paint in between uses.

You should remember to keep some kind of cover or plastic wrap on hand in order to preserve the paint that is on your palette. The paint is going to dry up quickly so you need to make sure to keep the paint wet and preserved when you are not using it right away. This is where the palette is able to come in handy because they will have all of the information and products that you need in order to keep the paints moist and ready to use.

If you have decided to mix large quantities of the paint all together, it is a good idea to come up with a palette that is going to have a small lid or cups in order to store the paint between your painting sessions. This helps you to better preserve these paints compared to covering the palette with some plastic wrap.

**Decide Painting Material**

One thing to remember about the acrylic paint is that it is very heavy and thick, which means that it can only be used on a couple of surfaces. You are not going to be able to use some basic paper and get the results that you are looking for. One of the most common surfaces that can be used for this kind of pant include treated wood, water color paper, canvas board, and stretched canvas. You should make sure that whatever kind of surface you are using for the painting that it is not very porous, that it is not oil, and that it is not greasy. If you are just starting out and you are worried about the way that the paint is going to start out, it is best to not start out with something that is really expensive. You can start out with some cheap watercolor paper and then once you get better at the process, you will be able to work your way up to using wood or a type of canvas.

**Gather the smaller items**

Now that you have taken the time to pick out some of the big items that you need in order to paint, you will need to choose some of the smaller items that can make this process easier.

Some examples of other tools that you might find useful will include a couple of jars to hold water, a palette knife, soap to clean out the brushes as you finish, a misting spray bottle that can hold the water, and an old cloth or rag to help clean up. You will be able to find all of these things at an art store, but you can also use some of the supplies that you have available at home if needed. You might also want to consider wearing an old shirt or a smock so that you do not have to worry about staining up your clothes with the paints and some old newspapers on the floor can prevent any accidents.

## Pick Location

Once you have all of the supplies that you plan on using for this project all laid out, you must choose the location where you would like to do the painting. As with many other activities, it is best to do this sort of painting in a nice natural light. You can set up the station for painting near a window that is open or choose another room in your home that has a lot of natural light. If possible, you might find that going outside is an option that can give great results. With this kind of light you will have a better chance seeing the different nuances of your colors and brush strokes that would be difficult to find and discover if you were in a bad light.

## Decide on the Subject

If you are new to painting, you will want make sure that you have a clear idea of your subject ahead of time. Some beginners may know exactly what they want to paint before they even get the materials while others are just excited to get started with the painting and might need some guidance about the things that they want to paint. There are endless possibilities about what you will be able to work with though it is often the easiest to work from a photograph or a 3D object that you will be able to see the object that is right in front of you rather than trying to do a mental picture that could make it difficult. If you are not able to pick out the first object that you would like to paint think about something that is simple such as a sunrise or a sunset, objects that are in your home, a vase of flowers, and a bowl of fruit.

## Start a sketch

Before you get started on the painting and start wasting away your paints hoping that it is just going to work out for you, it is a good idea to go through and create a rough sketch of the object that you plan to paint. This allows you to erase any mistakes that you are making easily and to determine if that object is going to work out the best for you without having to use any paint at all. This rough draft, when done, is going to help you gain the confidence that you need in order to paint the object exactly as you see it before jumping right into the painting. If you need to, it is possible to do a couple of different sketches before you begin painting. This allows you to try the object out in a couple of different lightings and in a different way and then you can decide which one you like the best compared to having to use all that paint to try out the object a few times. Once you have the sketch just as you like it, you can bring out the paints and get started.

## Mix the Paints

For many beginners, it is an easy mistake to make that you are mixing the paints as you work rather than doing the work to mix them all before you start the project. It is a lot more efficient and less time consuming to mix all of the paints and get the colors that you need before you start your painting. It is much better with acrylics to make more paint than you need and to mix them together for storage to use later if you need. If you only do a little bit and then try to mix them together again later, you may find that it is almost impossible to get the same color again. With the color palette that you chose, you will be able to properly store the pain to use at another time without having to worry about it being dried or ruined.

When you are mixing together your paints, it is better to use a color wheel. This can be a really helpful reference that can be used to mix together all of the paints. You will be able to use all of the basic colors in order to get the more specific colors that you want. If you find that mixing the colors together is not working in order to get exactly what you want, there are almost unlimited potential colors that you need at an art supply store and you can always use that as an option.

## Pick Light Source

Now that you have picked out all of the materials and gotten it all set up, you will need to take the time to find just the right light source that you need for your particular object. The color of the object is going to change depends on the way that your light hits the object, so before you start getting it all painted, you need to figure out where you are going to get your primary light source so that you are not ending up with different colors throughout the day. You should also pay more attention to the light all throughout the painting process; for example, you should make sure to have light colors that are nearer to your light source and then let the colors get darker when you are further away. This will also help to provide the depth that you need in order to make the picture look even better.

## Paint the Background First

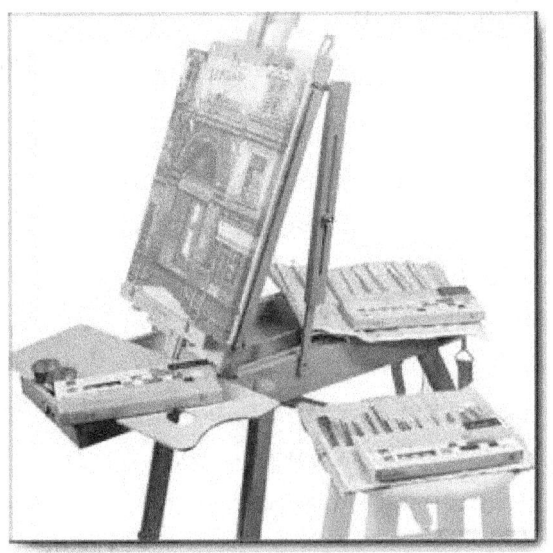

Often people will spend too much time just doing the main object of their composition and they are not going to think about the background until they are all the way done and it becomes much more difficult to accomplish. It is a much better idea for you to start with the background first. With acrylics you will be layering everything upwards, which means that you are going to be painting from the back of the picture to the front because this is the easiest. You should start with the medium value colors in the back and then follow this with your darkest colors and leave the brightest for the last in order to have the easiest application.

## Add the background details

Now that you are done with all of the background details and building up of your basic colors, I is important to add in some of the details of the background. If you are using a solid color, you should make sure to add in some shadows and other light points. If you have a background that has a pattern or that is very busy, you can add in some movement and texture using the brush strokes in order to complete the layer in the way that you want.

Image: Creative commons – Background painting

## Paint in the Other objects

There are a lot of other objects that you are going to add into the picture so this process can take some time to complete. You will want to work to break up the picture into the identifiable shapes that you want and then paint them in solid hues. As you work on building up the colors and the shapes, you are slowly going to begin to get your subject to appear. You should make sure to work in little section s at the time to make the process of painting a little less daunting as you go. As a beginner, you might find that it is easy to use a type of grid system when you are painting your subject. To do this, you can split up the canvas into different parts with an imaginary grid and then paint in that entire space of the grid until it is done before moving on to the next part of the grid. When it comes to your colors you need to make sure to do it in the right order. You should start out with the medium colors and then add on the darker colors before adding on the lighter colors. This can make the process easier to do because it can be hard to paint over your dark colors with one that is lighter so working your colors this way would be difficult.

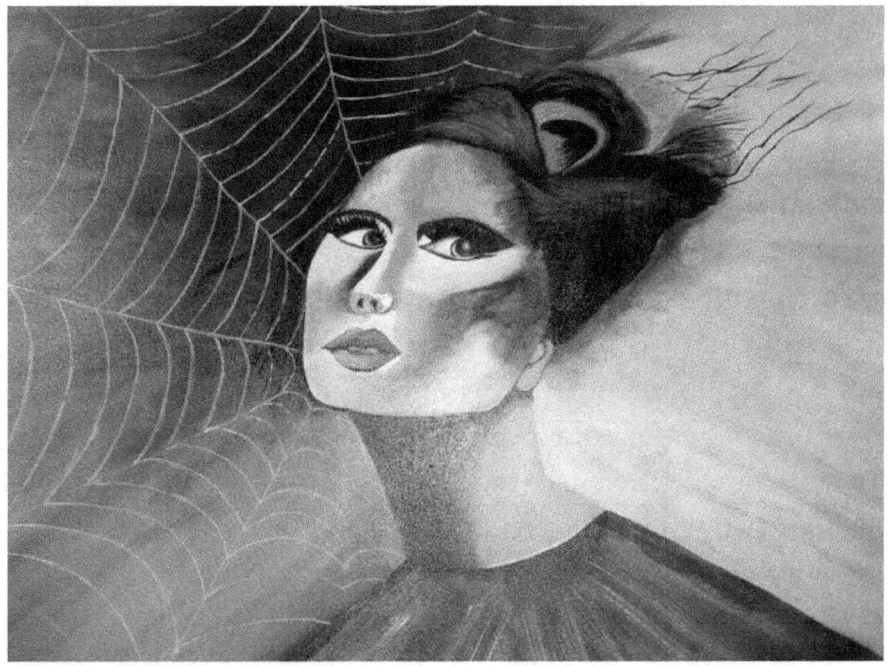

neruart. Deviantart

## Use different techniques for details

When you have taken the time to add in the basic shapes and colors that you want, it is time to add in the details that are needed. It is a good idea to use some different techniques of painting when you are working on these details. These will each help to focus on the movement and the texture that you want on your details based on the color applications and the paint brush strokes that you are using.

There are a lot of different techniques that you can use. If you stipple on the paint by taking the paint brush and holding it vertically before tapping onto the paper will give you the appearance of a lot of little dots without having to do each dot individually. This process is going to work best with a dry paint brush that has just a little bit of paint on it. If you are looking to get an unedited look to the paint that is rough and uses a broad stroke of color, you will find that painting with a palette knife can be useful. For this you will take the knife and coat it in a layer of paint before moving it over the canvas in order to load it up with the thick layers of the textured paint. The other method that you can try out is to create a wash of color simply by using water to thin out the paint. This method is able to give you a similar effect to watercolors where the paint will slowly lighten up on the canvas. If you are trying to create a gradation effect, this is the method to use.

**Finish the Painting**

You will want to add in a lot of details to your painting in order to get it to look the way that you want. You should spend a lot of attention on the subject matter, making sure to notice anything possible in order to add those finishing details that are necessary to make the painting perfect. This will sometimes include final dabs of dark and light as well as some of the outlines that you like to include as well as finishing up the washes of color.

**Add on some varnishing**

Now that you have done all of the work of adding in the details and the right colors to your painting, there are some finishing touches that you can consider adding in to your painting to make it perfect. One of these additions is to add in some varnish to your painting. This is not something that is really required, but a lot of painters like to add in a nice coat of varnish in order to finish up the picture and to seal in the paints. This is a great step to do because it helps to the canvas and the paint to chemically bond and will help to protect your painting from the damage.

## Clean up the work station

It is never a good idea to stop painting and then leave everything out. This is going to leave a huge mess and your paints are going to be ruined so that you are not able to use them again. Unless you are planning to buy new equipment and pain each time that you want to paint, you will need to clean up your area and our paint brushes immediately after you are done using them. The acrylic paint is able to severely damage and then ruin the paint brushes that you have if you let it stay and dry on top of the bristles. It is a good idea to wash out your brushes with some soap and cold water until the water begins to run clear. It is not a good idea to use warm or hot water because this will cause the paint to set in the brushes. You should also take the time to wipe up any of the paint that is on  your painting surface and rinse out the jars with some water.

## Save Unused Paint

Acrylic paint that is stored correctly can be saved for at least several months. You will be able to save it if you leave the paint in a container that is air tight. If you finish up your painting and you have some of the paint left, it is a good idea to set it aside to use later for some new pictures rather than wasting it and throwing it out. To save, bring out the containers with lids, scoop the paint into the containers, and place in a safe location.

**Let Painting Dry**

You need to give your painting some time to dry before you mess with it too much; if you touch it or get it all smudged too early, you will find that the painting is going to be ruined. You need to find a safe location where your painting is able to dry for at least a couple of days without being disturbed. These kinds of paints are able to dry really quickly, but it is still important that you leave them in a place where they will not be bothered so that they are able to cure.

**Show it Off**

This is one of the fun parts of your painting. You have put in a lot of time and effort to your project and now it is time to show it off and get the appreciation that you deserve. Find a place in your home or in your office where you are able to showcase the painting so that others are able to see what you have done. You can just simply hang it up in your home or get it matted and framed on a canvas or paper board to give it a new look. The decision for how you display the work is all up to you, but make sure that others are able to see and admire your work.

These are the steps that you should take if you really want to get into acrylic painting. There might seem like a lot of steps, but these are the things that you are going to need to do no matter what kind of paint that you are working with and most of them are pretty easy to understand. You will need to make sure that you are picking out the right kinds of equipment as well as the right colors. The object is important as well and sometimes the one that you choose is going to be determined by the skill level that you have. Even with all of these steps that you need to do in order to be successful, it is important to remember that the most critical step to follow is the one to have fun!

# Acrylic Painting Techniques

Acrylic paints are known for having shorter drying times as compared to oil paints. It is said that in less than ten minutes, acrylic paints dry up. In addition, they are also known for being soluble in water. Because of the distinct features that acrylic paints possess, many different styles of working with them have developed over time. Artists have found different ways of manipulating acrylic paints and turning them into beautiful, creative materials for artwork making. Each of these different techniques can be important because they are going to create something that is different in your painting and if you are able to use several different ones in the same painting, you are going to end up with something that is completely different. This variety of styles is called *acrylic painting techniques*. Some of the most common are the following:

*Creating fluid paints.* Although acrylic paints are different from watercolors, they can be used like watercolors, too. This is done by creating fluid paints. It is a technique in which water is added into and mixed with the paint in order to create a more fluid texture. However, mixing water and paint is not as easy as it seems. It requires appropriate proportion in order to achieve the shade and texture that you wish. If paint is greater than water, you will produce an opaque glaze. If you desire a smoother texture and produce a translucent glaze, there should be slightly greater water then the opaque, but must not be fifty percent greater than the paint otherwise, it will not stick to the canvas.

*Glaze Painting.* Glaze painting is a technique used to change the chroma, value, hue, and texture of a surface. Doing so makes a painting appear more realistic. It creates more depth in an image. There are different effects produced through glaze painting, reflecting how the lightness and darkness in shading affects the overall quality of the painting. Glazes can be made by artists themselves, and can also be brought as pre-mixed glazes. If you are trying to get a more natural look out of your object in the painting, you might find that using glaze painting is the way to go.

*Pouring Paints.* The mainstream manner of painting is by using tools such as brushes. Some painters, however, have discovered a new exciting way of creating a wonderful artwork, which is through pouring paints. Acrylic paints are poured directly on the canvass, and they are manipulated by tilting the canvas until the paints move and blend naturally. It is an innovative painting technique because it has developed beyond the conventional way that most artists use in painting. Pouring paints can be done with either just one color or with multiple colors to allow for color blending.

*Dry Brushing.* This is an acrylic painting technique that uses only small amounts of paint. Using a dry brush, the painter scrubs layers of colors onto the canvass. Strokes are added in the same manner as how colored pencils are applied. This can give a unique look to your paintings because the strokes can give you the thin lines that are desirable from color pencils but you will still be able to get the bright colors that are desirable from the acrylic paint.

*Dabbing.* This acrylic painting technique is used in adding texture to your painting. One common use of dabbing is when the painter creates bushes or textures on the ground. A stiff bristle brush is used in a pouncing motion. Multiple layers are commonly used in order to build depth in the image. Depending on how you want the texture to be, the brush may be dry or the paint may be slightly mixed with water.

*Sponging.* Sponging is done through the same manner as dabbing, however the material used is different. Aside from a stiff bristle brush, a piece of sponge is used. It gives a unique texture that is difficult to achieve with the use of mere brushes. Through sponging, irregular patterns are produced. Sponging is something different that you can use in your painting that helps to show some movement in your work or adds in a little something different to the texture that you are not able to get in other ways.

*Detailing.* As we all know, there are different types of brushes with varying sizes used in painting. In this acrylic painting technique, a smaller and more pointed brush is used to specific details. Detailing requires focus because lines must be clear, shapes are supposed to be definite, and edges should be precise. Detailing is preferred if the painter wants to create a more definite image. Detailing is something that is going to take a lot of extra effort to accomplish because there are just so many little things that you have to pay attention to in order to get it right. This method of concentrating can be really difficult for beginners who are not used to it.

*Underpainting.* Underpainting means quickly laying out visible information of the painting. It is like a draft in which light shades are used, because they serve as a guide, as well as an initial background of your painting. You do not need to be very detailed or conscious about doing it perfectly because you only need to add the shadows, highlights and basic colors. This is a step that you can take after you have drawn out your sketch because you will get the little details out of the way ahead of time and the spend more time on the important things later.

*Scumbling.* This technique is basically brushing broken and thin layers of paint over another. By doing so, bits of the lower layers show. Aside from adding depth, it also gives variation of color. Scumbling often gives an effect of an optical illusion, but you will see the scumbled layer as you look at the painting from a closer distance. For a painting that needs to have some layering added in, scumbling is the method that you should use.

*Stippling.* This technique makes use of the ends of the bristles on a brush to create small spots. The result is an illusion of grain. These small dots create varying degrees of solidity and shading. Patterns created through stippling are commonly seen in paintings involving nature. It is said to be very helpful in painting leaves of trees and plants. In some cases you may find that stippling can create some more texture in your painting compared to using the straight lines and brush strokes. If you are looking to do something that is like pointillism but do not want to go through quite the effort that is needed with each individual dot, the stippling method can sometimes help since it is going to give you a lot of little dots all at once.

*Spraying.* This is another acrylic painting technique that results to a "grain" effect, but with the use of toothbrushes, or materials alike. A toothbrush, for example, is dipped in paint, and the finger is used to brush through it, allowing it to spray paints into the canvass. The effect, however, can be quite messy, but it can also be fun. This is a good method to use if you are trying to give a kind of messy look to the painting or you are interested in adding something that is a little bit out there to your work.

Mentioned above are just some of the commonly used acrylic painting techniques. A lot of artists all over the world use many more techniques that seem quite complicated to beginners. For now, these are the basic techniques that you should know to help you get started. These techniques are helpful to help you achieve the painting that you dream of, that is why knowing them better and practicing them from time to time is a necessity. After some time of practice, you will eventually get the hang of it. When you do, it is easier for you to create more wonderful paintings that will bring you closer to your dream of becoming a great artist.

# Grades and Varieties of Acrylic Paint

A crylic paints can be categorized according to their grades and varieties. This allows painters to distinguish an acrylic paint from the other, giving them an idea of what acrylic paint is best used in their situation, as conditioned by their purpose or desired results. The three grades of commercial acrylic paint are the following:

*Artist or Professional Acrylics.* These acrylic paints are designed for professional artists. They are aimed at achieving the cleanest mixing results; therefore they are highly pigmented with a focus on single pigment colors. Their viscosity is somewhat similar to oil paints. Because of this, they are able to hold brush strokes for impasto applications.

*Student Acrylics.* These acrylic paints are designed for painters who are not yet veterans in the field. Student acrylics are somewhat similar to artist or professional acrylics, but they have lower pigment concentrations. They are usually less expensive than the artist or professional acrylics. Moreover, they come with a smaller range of colors and to achieve different shades and hues, colors are usually mixed, but the results are quite different from full-strength colors. This is a good place for you to start if you are looking to begin with this kind of painting. While there might be fewer options, they are going to be a little bit easier to use and will not cost you as much as some of the more professional options.

*Scholastic Acrylics.* This grade of acrylic paints is best suited for painters who are just getting started. Using less expensive pigments, young artists find this more efficient even if the color range is limited only to primary and secondary colors. Scholastic acrylics have drawbacks, however. Actual pigments are not specified and light fastness may be poor.

Acrylic paints can also be categorized by their varieties. The varieties of acrylic paints are the following:

*Craft Acrylics.* Aside from canvas, this variety of acrylics can be used on different surfaces such as wood, ceramics, and metals. As you look around your room, you recognize the use of craft acrylics. Their primary purpose is for decorative painting and faux finishes. They are less concentrated on paint pigments. It is easier to spread them quickly, but there is difficulty in attaining different textures.

*Open Acrylics.* The major difference between acrylic paints and oil paints is that acrylic paints take lesser time to dry. They can be completely dried up in less than ten minutes. To address this difference, open acrylics are produced. Thickness, temperature and humidity account for the length of time it will take for the paint to dry.

*Heavy Body Acrylics.* As its name states, this type of acrylics is best suited for heavy paint applications, including impasto applications. "Heavy" here refers to the thickness or viscosity of the paint. This type of paint is usually found in Artist or Professional Acrylics or Student Acrylics.

*Fluid Acrylics.* Fluid acrylics are the same with heavy body acrylics in terms of pigmentation, but are less viscous. They are best used for watercolor techniques, airbrush application, or if the painter wants smooth coverage.

*Interactive Acrylics.* This type of acrylics also possesses the fast drying characteristic of acrylic paints, but they allow for longer drying time if the painter needs more. These all-purpose artistic colors are best used for wet blending.

*Exterior Acrylics.* The paints you usually see outside your house are exterior acrylics. They are designed to resist outdoor conditions such as water and heat. They can also be applied to different kinds of surfaces. Exterior acrylics are best use for architectural murals, outdoor signs, and others.

Categorizing acrylics according to grade and variety is one way to distinguish what paint is better to use in different circumstances. Having an idea of the different grades and varieties of acrylic paint helps the painter choose the appropriate paint that he or she would need. Being able to do so will gives one's work a better quality. Different kinds of acrylics paints serve different purposes. If those purposes correspond to yours, then you should make use of that paint. Not doing so may result to a poor quality of your work, or failure to achieve the artwork you desired. The information above will help you distinguish an acrylic paint from the other, as well as which of them is best suited for your masterpiece.

# Acrylic Painting Tips for Beginners

Now that you are equipped with the basic knowledge about acrylic painting and acrylic paints, specifically techniques, grades, and variations, you are now ready to get your hands on your paint and canvas. However, there are a few tips and reminders that you should keep in mind. Upon knowing these tips and reminders, you will be guided throughout your acrylic painting activity. This chapter will introduce to you these things to help you get started. They are as follows:

*Keep Your Acrylic Paints Workable.* As mentioned earlier, acrylic paints only take a little time to dry up. In just a couple of minutes, they are no longer wet. To keep your entire set of acrylic paints workable, you need to keep it from drying up entirely. You can do this by keeping it capped when not in use, and by squeezing only little amounts when you are using it. It is important to keep your acrylic paints moist and usable, so that you will be refrained from buying new sets over and over again. Maintaining the workability of your acrylic paints allows you to maximize their use, and makes your painting activity less costly. Refrain from pouring large amounts of paint on sheets of paper, because they will tend to dry up in no time. You will only be wasting your acrylic paints and you will be forced to buy again. To have an efficient and inexpensive painting activity, keep your acrylic paints workable.

*Blot Your Paint Brushes.* It takes time and effort to wipe your brushes after rinsing them off. Sometimes, people do not rinse their brushes off properly. Experts advise that you make it a habit to wipe your brushes on a piece of paper towel or cloth after rinsing them. This is to keep your brushes neat and free from excess paints that were not rinsed off properly. Not being able to do so will leave paint on your brushes, causing colors to mix and preventing you from achieving the exact shade and mixture of colors that you want. When this happens, the tendency is to produce blotches that are not good for your painting. Keeping your brushes clean at all times prevents these kinds of problems from happening.

*Prepare the materials beforehand.* It is important to prepare your materials before you start painting so that you can concentrate on creating your art piece. Having to run out for more materials will distract you from what you need to do. Basically, what you will need are brushes, palette, surfaces, and water container. Professionals suggest that brushes that are made from synthetic materials such as nylon are best suited for acrylic paints. Thick painting is best done with stiff brushes. Thinned painting is made through the use of soft paintbrushes. You will also need a palette that is flat and impervious to water. Since acrylics dry quickly, there are available plastic palettes that have lids or sealable compartments that are designed to prevent acrylic paints from drying. Palettes that absorb water, such as wood, must be avoided. Any stable and non-greasy surface can be used for acrylic painting. This is one of the best features of acrylic paints – they can be applied on almost any surface. There are, however, preferred ones. These include artist's canvas, hardboard, heavy watercolor paper, and fiberboard. Any water container, as long as it is large and unbreakable, is perfect for your painting activity.

*Change the water frequently.* This may also require some time and effort but it pays off. As you work on your painting, you make use of different colors of acrylic paint. Because of this, the water is tinted with different colors. Unless, of course, you have separate water containers in which to rinse different paint colors. It is important to change the water frequently so that the brush will be clean and clear for the next color of acrylic paint that you will use. By doing so, unintended mixing of colors can be avoided. It will also prevent you from messing up your work.

*Basic precautions should be taken.* One of the best features of acrylic paints is that it is safe to use. However, some components of acrylic paints are toxic. It is important to take some basic precautionary measures when handling acrylic paint. Be reminded to keep the paint away from your eyes, mouth and lungs. Paints have the ability to damage your organs if you do not use them with proper caution. It is also important to wash your hands thoroughly after your painting activity. It is noted previously that one of the techniques used in acrylic painting is splashing. To keep everything safe, it would be better to use eye protection when using this technique. For the safety of everyone, keep the materials away from children. Not keeping these reminders in mind may cause accidents. Carelessness invites danger that is why it is important to behave safely at all times.

*Buy the less expensive acrylic paints.* Since you are just getting started, you can settle for the less expensive grades of acrylics. You can use the more expensive ones when you are finally getting the hang of acrylic painting, and when you are ready to take on a more challenging painting activity. Even if they are of lesser quality, they are best suited for young artists. Expensive acrylics will only go to waste if non-professionals who have no background about how to use them properly and effectively use them. Do not worry, because eventually, after some time of practice, you will be capable of handling expensive and professional acrylic paints. For the mean time, settle with the less expensive ones.

*Blend colors quickly.* Blending is necessary if you want to achieve a better quality of your artwork. However, this is not very easy to do with acrylic paints. Acrylic paints dry quickly that is why blending colors must be done quickly as well. It might be difficult at first, and you might experience a lot of drying up during your first few tries, but you will learn to do it properly after some time. Practicing regularly how to blend with acrylic paints will help you find it easier for yourself the next time that you engage in a painting activity.

*Select a good location.* It is best to paint with natural light. Well-lighted areas of your home are the best locations to do your artwork. You can usually fin these near an open window or a room equipped with natural light. Painting in a poorly lighted area will cause you to produce unintended results. The tendency is for some details to be hidden, and unnecessary elements be unseen. When this happens, your artwork will become poor in quality. You will suddenly notice mistakes that you did not see while you were painting, because the area is poorly lighted. Natural lighting gives you the ability to see your work properly, allowing you to spot, if not avoid mistakes immediately.

*Make sure your paints are closed properly*. It is important to make sure that the lids and covers of your acrylic paints are screwed on tightly at all times to keep them from drying up. When this happens, your acrylic paints will be put to waste. Even if they are not that expensive, it is important to keep them closed properly in order to maximize its use. Always put the covers back immediately after use.

*Keep your materials in a good place*. When you are finally done with your painting activity, clean all your materials up and gather them together. Sort them accordingly. Paintbrushes must be grouped together. The same goes for acrylic paints, sponges, palettes, and other materials. Make sure that you keep them in a room or container with a not so low and not so high temperature. This will help your materials to keep their quality and to keep them usable for future use. Failure to do so will cost you more because you would have to buy the materials again.

*Transparent vs. Opaque colors*—there are many different colors that you will be able to choose when you are doing acrylic painting. It is all going to depend on how you want each of your paintings to turn out. If you want the opaque variation of your colors, you should apply it thickly and straight out of the tube without any water added to the pain. Sometimes you will be able to add it in with a little bit of titanium what since this is going to work with all of the different colors in order to make hem opaque. On the other hand, if you are trying to dilute the color and make it look more like you are airbrushing or that you are using watercolors, a little bit of water, or a lot if you really want to make it light, will do the trick.

*Acrylic vs. watercolor for washing*—when you are using this paint, you will find that when acrylic dries it becomes permanent and you are not going to be able to make any changes to the finished work. On the other hand, if you use a watercolor wash with your project, it will become insoluble and you will be able to wash over it with paint without making any disturbances in the existing wash. With the watercolor wash, the colors of all the subsequent washes are going to mix optically with the ones that you did earlier. A watercolor glaze can also be lifted off with a cloth and some water. It is a good idea to figure out how you would like the painting to end up ahead of time so that you are able to choose the right wash on the paint.

These are just some of the tips and reminders that will help you to get started. Professional artists advise that you keep them in mind while you are just beginning, and even if you have already come a long way in your painting venture. They will be useful every time you engage in acrylic painting. It will not only help maintain the quality of your materials, it will also allow you to enjoy a hassle-free and worthwhile activity.

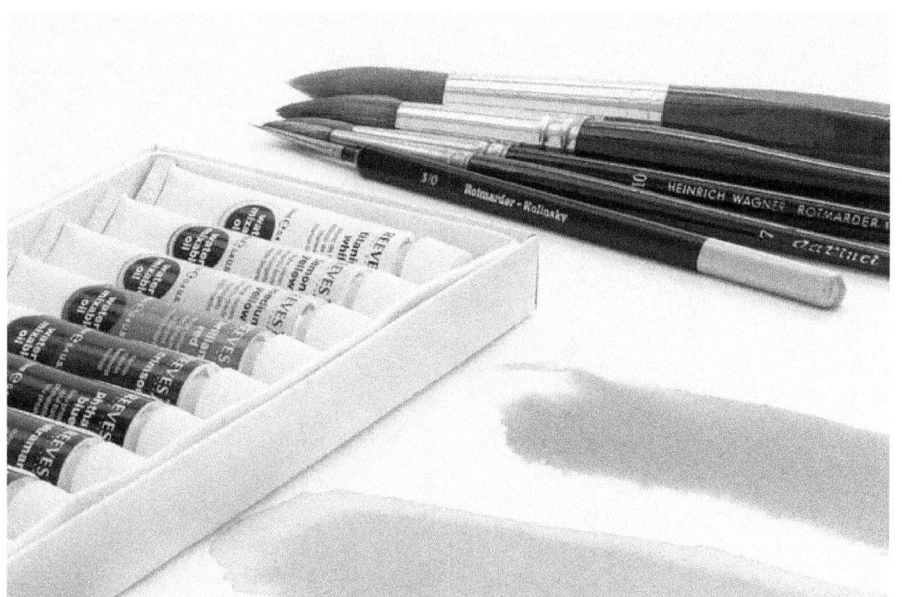

# Cleaning Your Acrylic Paints

Once you have taken the time to make your masterpiece, which is sure to have taken a lot of thought and work up to this point, you are sure to be feeling pretty great. These kinds of paints will dry quickly so you are going to get a pretty good idea of how the final product is going to look fairly soon after you are done with all of the work. You should feel proud; it takes a lot of time and effort in order to get the painting to look just the way that you want it and even the process of mixing the paints to get the just right effect is going to take some time and concentration. But now that you are done with all of this, it is important that you do not forget one important last step—to clean up your work station and all of your supplies. This chapter is going to discuss how you can do this so that it is done right and you do not end up ruining any of your supplies.

## Clean Up Area

As soon as you are done with your painting, it is a good idea to clean up. You should not leave a mess behind because the longer that the mess is there the longer it is going to take in order to get it clean and after so much time you are not going to be able to get it cleaned up at all. Make sure to put all of your paints away, through away anything that you are not going to use again, and wipe down any of the surfaces that might have gotten paint on them. It is also a good idea to put everything away so that it does not end up getting ruined before you are able to use again.

## Paint Brushes

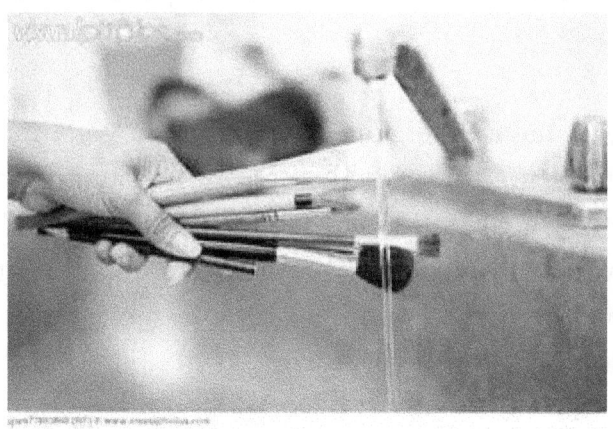

The first thin that you will need to do is work on the paint brushes. You will want to make sure that you are spending some extra time on these because if they are not cleaned out completely, you are going to have brushes that are ruined. For those who have spent a lot of money on the supplies and gotten some really nice brushes, this is not something that you want to see happen. So what you will do is bring the brushes to the sink and turn on some cold water. Rinse up the brushes under this cold water, making sure to work the bristles of the brush around and get to separating them out so that they are not holding on to any of the paint. Once the paint dries into the brushes, they are going to be ruined because you will not be able to get it out later like you can with some of the other types of paint and acrylic paints dry really quickly so this can be a big concern. One thing to keep in mind with this step is that you must use cold water; warm water is just going to cause the paints to dry more quickly and be more likely to harm your brush.

While the brushes are still underwater, make sure to take some extra time to get all of the paint removed. There is a good chance that the paint is going to get stuck under some of the bristles so that you need to move them all around. One way that you can tell that the paint brushes are getting clean is to run the water over them. If the water is running with color, than there is still paint inside. If there is just clear water, they are clean. You should do this a few time and move around the bristles until you are sure that there is no paint left in them.

Once the water is running clear for you, it is a good idea to use some soap to clean them out even more, just in case. There are some special brush conditioning soaps that you can use that will help out a lot, but they are not necessary. You can simply use a regular type of hand soap that has some conditioner in it if you would like to save a little money or if you do not have any of the other kind on hand. Scrub the conditioner of your choice into the paint brushes and then make sure to rinse it out completely so that no more bubbles are coming out.

Next, take the paint brushes out of the water and wipe them dry with a clean towel. Make sure that the towel you are using is not one of them that you had used during the whole painting process. Doing this is going to make it more likely that more paint is going to get back on the paint brushes and can ruin all the work that you are doing. After you have wiped the paint brushes dry, you need to shape them back into their form. This can either be done by hand or by using a brush shaper.

Now that the paint brushes are starting to look better and the way that they are supposed to, you need to let them have some time to dry out from the water. Pick out a clean area to lay them down. Now that the paint is all out of them a clean counter would work fine or you can lay them down on a clean towel or other clothe. It will take a little bit of time for the paint brushes to get completely dry so you can just leave them there for now.

Once the paint brushes have had time to air dry for a while, it is important that you put them away. It is never a good idea to leave the paint brushes out in the open where they could get contaminated and ruin the paint and your picture later on or where they might get ruined by other things. After the paint has had time to dry, place them back in wherever you would like to store them until they are ready to be used again. This could be a painting drawer or some other container that you have specifically set aside in order to make sure that they are not bothered by other things.

All of this might seem like it is a lot of work in order to get cleaned up, but it is really necessary that you take care of your paint brushes unless you would like to spend a lot of money replacing them each time that you were ready to paint. These kinds of paints are really good at sticking on to the paint brush and since they dry really quickly, if you do not take the time to get them cleaned off right away, the paint is never going to go away. Proper cleaning and maintenance of your painting tools is essential to giving you the exact right picture each time.

## Cleaning Off Clothes

There are times when these kinds of paints are going to try and stick to your clothes. It is easy to drip some onto you or you might even lean up against the picture at some point during your work. For the most part, it is a good idea to make sure that you wear some sort of artists outfit or some other articles of clothing that you will not mind getting dirty or ruined while you are painting. But there are times when you might be done with painting and you brush up against it before it has had time to dry or even someone else might brush up against it before you are done with the painting. If this is something that does happen, you would not want to be stuck with them on there forever and possible never get to wear that outfit again. This section is going to talk a little bit about what you can do if you get acrylic paints on your clothes and how you could get them out.

If you do end up in the situation where you get this kind of paint on your clothes, it is important to take care of the stain right away and get it all washed out. You will want to get this done while the stain is still wet; otherwise, it is too late to get it out. Bring out a little bit of soapy water, rub it well, and then make sure and rinse completely. If the paint is still really difficult to get off the article of clothing, it is a good idea to try out some spray spot remover or some washer detergent and then rub the spot with a toothbrush. It is not a good idea to give the paint any time in order to sink into the fabric or to dry. Once this does happen, it is pretty much impossible to get the stain out at all and you may be stuck with it for the long term. As stated, if you would like to avoid any of the stress that comes from getting paint on your clothes, it is a good idea to wear an outfit that you do not care if it gets ruined or not. This is going to allow you the freedom to enjoy your artwork rather than worrying about what you are wearing.

If this is not working, there are other things that you can try out in order to get it all cleaned off. First, you should take a cotton ball or two and place it into some rubbing alcohol in order to soak. It is best if you are able to get it completely saturated because there is not an issue with being to much of the liquid. Nail polish remover or some paper towels will also work out well. Bring out the article of clothing that has the stain and dab the paint spots with this cotton ball. You will want to make sure that the area with the stain on the fabric is getting soaked all the way through with the rubbing alcohol so that it is able to work through deep into the fibers and then loosen up the paint. Now you should be able to wipe the paint away. Keep using the cotton ball in order to dab the paint until it starts to come off. Try to work at not spreading the paint into new areas as you are wiping and be extra gentle if you are using delicate fabrics such as silk. If you are using these kinds of fabrics, it is a good idea to blot rather than scrub at the stain. Keep adding more of the rubbing alcohol and dabbing until the stain is gone and there are no more traces of the color.

Once you have gotten to this point, you will need to launder the garment. Use some of your regular laundry detergent and get the item of clothing completely clean. Also, follow the regular instructions in order to dry the article as well. Once the item of clothing is cleaned, you can check the spot that was the stain. At this point, it should not be possible to see the paint stain anymore. If you are still able to see the stain, it is important that you repeat this process and get some more of the paint out of the stain before cleaning again.

## Cleaning Off Palette

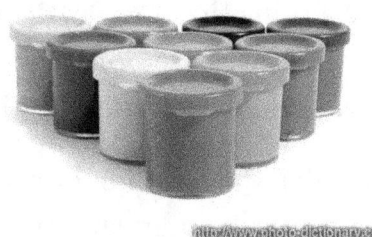

http://www.photo-dictionary.com

While you are painting your next masterpiece, you are sure to be using a palette of some sort in order to hold your paints while you are going. This is a great idea, but you may be wondering what you are going to do when you are done in order to clean up the palettes. There are a few different types of palettes that you could be using for your project and the one that you are using is going to determine what you can do in order to get it cleaned off. This section is going to discuss how you would clean off both a wooden palette, a ceramic, glass, or plastic palette, and a paper palette so that you are all set and taking care of it in the right way.

The first type of palette that we will discuss is the wooden palette. It is usually not recommended that you use this type of palette when you are using acrylic paints simply because it is so porous. This means that the wood is going to absorb the paint and make it really difficult in order to get the paint out of there. Often the palette is going to become stained or ruined because the paint is going to dry before you are able to get it all cleaned out. Often the best choices to use for this kind of painting are ones that do not have pores such as ceramic and glass as well as plastic. If you are using a wood palette and do not want to spend money on a new one, the best thing that you can do is wrap it with some plastic wrap. Then when you are done you will be able to just throw the plastic away and the palette will still be in good shape.

The next type of palettes that you might be interested in using for this type of painting include ceramic, glass, and plastic. These are great options because you will be able to use them without worrying about any pores getting in the way or the paint getting stuck. Any of the leftover paint that is still on one of these palettes should never be washed down your sink drain. These kinds of paints are considered to be very polluting to the environment so other methods of cleaning up are often recommended and preferred. What you can do if you are using one of these kinds of palettes is to bring out a paper towel and get it a little bit wet. Wipe the palette off with this paper towel before throwing it into the trash. Once the palette is all wiped up, you can place it into the sink and then wash it off with some soapy water. You will want to make sure to scrub all areas and corners of the palette to ensure all of the water is gone. While it is best to clean off the palette while the paint is still wet, it is possible to get some of the pain off even if it has had time to dry. If the paint has dried on this kind of palette, you will be able to just pull it off before throwing away. This is because the paint is going to dry into a type of rubbery layer when it is on one of these kinds of palettes. If you find that it is really difficult to get the paint off from one of these kinds of palettes, it is a good idea to spray on some kind of window cleaner, such as Windex and then let the palette set for a few minutes. Then the paint should just slide right off for you.

The third type of palette that you might consider using for this project is a paper palette. This is a very popular form of palette anymore because it allows the artist to use the paints and then just dispose of the whole palette when they are done without having to worry about any of the clean up. It is possible to purchase these kinds of tablets with waterproof paper sheets that are the disposable part if you do not want to throw the whole palette away each time. Then you are only needing to dispose of the top part. With the disposable paper palettes, it is possible to eliminate all of the issues that might come with cleaning up acrylic paints and anything that might happen when the paints mix with the waterways, which is what will often happen when you are cleaning up a palette.

With all of these palettes, timing is one of the most important things that you have to keep track of. You do not want to wait around and save the cleaning up process to do sometime in the future. It is something that needs to be done right away before the paint has any time to dry up. If you get done with the painting, you should turn around and start cleaning up your palettes because the sooner that you are able to do this the better. Never let this kind of paint dry up or you run the risk of never being able to get it cleaned up at all. If you have to delay the cleaning process for some reason, it is a good idea to keep the spot that you must clean up wet. You can place a cloth on it or just find another way in order to keep it wet. This will help to prevent the paint from drying up and it will in turn remain water soluble so that you are able to clean it up later.

**Removing From Carpet**

There may be some instances when you get some of this kind of paint on your carpet. This can be a big pain because you will have to do a lot of scrubbing and you do not want to be stuck with the decision to leave the carpet how it is or replace the whole room. Here are some of the steps that you can take in order to get this kind of paint off your carpet.

First, you are going to need to bring out some rubbing alcohol and place a lot of it on the spot where the stain is. You will want this area to soak and it needs to be completely saturated before you go on to the next step. Allow this rubbing alcohol to sit on the area for at least 5 minutes so that it has a chance to loosen up the paint. Once the five minutes are up, you can bring out a paper towel and blot the area with the stain. Try your best to not spread the paint to other areas of the carpet as you work on the blot; it is best if you are able to keep it all in one location in order to make sure that it is manageable. You will need to continue with this process of blotting and soaking until the paint is completely gone. This whole process might end up taking three or more soakings before you are able to get all of the paint to go away. Next, you can bring out your carpet cleaner and clean up the whole area. This is going to help you to get rid of any of the last traces of stain that are there. When the carpet is completely dried, it is going to be rid of the stain. This process might seem like it is going to take a bit, but it is the best way to ensure that you are getting your carpet back to normal when you are done.

**Removing From Wood**

At times, you may be forced to use a wood palette or some other wooden object might end up getting stained with the acrylic paint. This section is going to talk a little bit about the steps that you can take if this ends up happening so that you can get rid of the paint on the area.

First, you should bring out a sharp instrument and try to use it in order to pry the paint up. Since most types of wood are going to use some sort of shiny finish, it is best to try using a sort of prying method before you have to resort to using some form of a chemical. The best bet is to use a sharp knife and slowly place it under the edge of the paint splatter and use an attempt in order to pry it up. A few things to remember before you do this is that you should not angle the knife in a downward way or else you are going to scratch up the wood. If the paint is not willing to pop up easily, then it is time to try out another method; it is not a good idea to try and force this.

If the method above is not working out well for you, it is time to go on to another one. You will need to grab some soapy water and try to clean the paint from the area. You should make the solution one that is a combination of soap and some warm water and then pour it all over the area. Try to slowly scrub the stain away, taking some extra care not to get the wood all scratched up. Once you have done this for a bit, you can bring out the rubbing alcohol and soak up a corner of a paper towel that is folded in it. Gently rub on the surface that has the stain in order to try and get it off, taking some care to not get the substance on the wood. The paint should slowly start to loosen up a bit before transferring over to the paper towel. Continue to dab the area with the paper towel so that the paint can slowly end up dissolving. This method has a potential of damaging the wood finish in your home so you must use it carefully and try not to splatter the alcohol. Once you have gotten all of the paint removed, it is a good idea to take some time and clean up the area. Use a cleaner that is approved for wood flooring in order to clean up the area that became stained. Allow the floor some time to dry up completely. After these steps the area should be completely paint free.

There are many different surfaces that can get ruined by the painting that you are doing and since this kind of paint is one that is able to dry up quickly, it is important that you take the time to learn how to clean up any of the messes that are made. This chapter went through quite a few different instances when you might make a stain in your home or your life and some step by step instructions that you are going to be able to follow in order to make it all better and cleaned up. Use them any time that you are potentially going to make a mess in order to avoid any of the stresses that might come.

# How to Keep Acrylic Paints from Drying Out

One of the most difficult things that you will have to deal with when you are working with these kinds of paints is how you are going to keep them from drying out. Once the acrylic paints dry all up, they are stuck that way and you will not be able to use them again. This chapter is going to take some time to talk about how you can keep your acrylic paints wet as well as how you should store the paints between your painting sessions.

## Keeping Acrylic Paints Wet

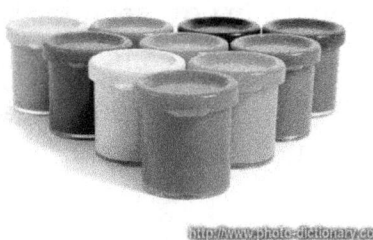

http://www.photo-dictionary.com

The first thing that you could consider doing is to purchase a special palette that is meant to keep these kinds of paints wet. There are several different brands that are going to provide you with the right kind of palette as well as a special sponge that is designed in order to keep the paper wet on the palette, which is in turn going to keep the paint workable for a much longer period of time.

If you do not want to spend a lot of money on a palette, you can choose one of the many different homemade alternatives. Even though you will be making them at home, they are going to work in the same way that the wet palette does. If you do construct your own, it is a good idea to make sure that the surface is not getting too wet. If you do allow it to get too wet, then you are dealing with the issue of the paint absorbing the water and then becoming really runny.

Another option that people like to go with is to use a spray. What you would do with this option is bring out a spray bottle with some water. Then, every once in a while when you are painting, you will then spray the paints with the water in order to keep them moist and to prevent any drying out. This is kind of like a misting approach and it can do a great job at keeping the paints workable. But it is going to take some time and some experience in order to figure out how much of the spraying needs to be done in order to get the paints to work again.

The final option that you can go with is to use one of the newer acrylics that are being developed. These types are ones that have been developed in order to be workable for a longer period of time. They can have an extended life span from a day to a whole week depending on the type of working conditions that you are dealing with as well as the brand that you purchase. This can help you out because you are going to have a longer amount of time in order to make the perfect painting that you want.

Some of the other things that you can do in order to make sure that your paints are staying moist like you would enjoy. These include:

- Tin foil and plastic pots—there are some people who believe that using these little plastic pots or some tin foil on top of them can help to keep the moisture into the paints rather than in the air. It is a good idea to place in a little dab of the water to the paint in order to keep them wet. If you do add in this little bit of water, it is a good idea to use it within a few days so that you are not getting mold to show up.
- Carry out containers—another option that you can choose in order to keep your paints moist or to store them is to use things like carry out containers. Wax paper and shipping foam are also going to work out well. These are nice because you are able to close up the lids nice and tight so you do not have to worry about the moisture getting out. These containers are able to help with the wet sponge effect, especially if you are able to add in some waxed paper on top of the wet foam in the palette. You might also find that doing an occasional mist every few days until you use up the paint can help as well.
- Dinner plate with wet tissue—if you have some nice porcelain white dinner plates, you may be able to use them as a type of palette and it is going to be easy to

clean off because there are no pores to worry about. If you want to keep the paint out for a little bit longer while you are working without having to worry about the issues with drying, you can take some tissue and then soak it in some water. Squeeze out the excess water and then leave it along the edge of the plate. This is going to provide the moisture that your paints need in order to stay wet. If you end up having to stop painting for a bit with this method, you can just bring out another plate and place it over the first one in order to keep the plates dry.

- Glass dish and rubber lid—it is possible to use some of your glass dishes with some rubber lids in order to keep the paint nice and moist like you would like. Before you start painting, you can place a paper towel down in the dish, making sure to cover up the whole bottom and then lightly wet the paper towel. Then take some plastic food wrap and place it on top of the paper towel in order to use a palette. When you are done, place the lid on top and your paints should be ready to go for the next two weeks.

- Ice cube trays—this is a great way for you to keep the paints wet and moist while also holding them into their own place so that they do not get mixed. When you are done with the paints and want to store them, all that you are going to need to do is cover up the ice cube trays with some plastic wrap.

- Plastic Syringes—you know those big syringes that are given out at the doctor's office or in the pharmacy that help you or your children to take the medicine that you need? It is possible to use those in order to store and preserve your own paints, especially when it comes to using colors that you mixed. What you are going to do is mix up the colors and then such them inside a syringe of your choice. You can use a couple of different ones for each color. Then you will dispense them when you need instead of using all at once.

- Plastic cups—the final thing that you can do is to bring out a plastic cup. While you are painting, you can make sure to place all of the paints inside of a plastic cup, making sure to spray them a few times to keep them moist. When you are done with the painting for the day, make sure that the paint inside of the cups are well moistened and then you can set these cups upright in an airtight container. After it is all done, you can seal up the container and place in a safe area. This will allow you to keep the paints good for up to three months as long as it is done in the right manner.

## How to Store Paints

One of the options that you have for storing your paints is to just use them all up when you are done with the painting. With this method, you are just going to take out the amount of paint that you need and then use it all up in the one sitting rather than trying to save it for another painting session. This allows you to not worry about if the paint is going to stay well for the next time that you want to paint and you can also get a fresh start each time that you are painting. One thing that you need to keep in mind is that you might waste a lot of paint in the beginning because you might not be used to the amount of paint that you are going to use. Over time, you will learn this and be able to keep the waste down to the minimum.

There are other times when you might need to save your paint for another time. You might decide that you do not want to waste out the extra paint that you poured out or you worked really hard in order to get a particular color or a shade of color that you would like to save it to work on later rather than trying to get that same color later in. If this is true of yours, you might need to purchase a special sponge type palette. With these palettes, you will be able to place the paints inside and then have them stay workable for a week or so. This is one of the best ways to make sure that the paints are staying well for storage until you are able to use them again.

# Famous Acrylic Painters and Their Works

Now that you know the basic techniques, materials, tips, and reminders necessary for young and aspiring artists like you, it is time that you get yourselves some inspiration. This chapter will introduce to you some of the famous acrylic painters and their works. Learn from their techniques and experiences!

## Andy Warhol

Andrew "Andy" Warhol was born on August 6, 1928 in Pittsburgh, Pennsylvania. He became a leading artist of the 1960's pop art movement after being a successful magazine and ad illustrator. He was great acrylic painter, but other than that, he was also engaged in performance art, video installations, writing, and filmmaking. He spent his education in Carnegie Institute, Schenley High School, and Carnegie Institute for Technology. On the 22$^{nd}$ of February 1987, Andy died in New York.

Andy Warhol's artistic life began in 1949 when he graduated from college with his Bachelor of Fine Arts degree. He began as a commercial artist. He had a job in a magazine company and became on the most successful commercial artists of his time, exemplified by the number of awards he earned. After his career in that magazine company, he began focusing his attention to painting. He emphasized on the concept of pop art. His paintings of Campbell's soup cans brought Warhol and pop art into the national spot light for the first time. Warhol is known for his paintings that depicted hamburger, Coca-cola bottles, and vacuum cleaners. Marilyn Monroe, Mick Jagger, Elizabeth Taylor, and Mao Zedong also became the subjects of his paintings. The painting that became a hit during his time was his portrait Eight Elvises.

Warhol's creativity and passion in painting resulted to the creation of "The Factory", which was his own art studio. It is a large silver-painted warehouse that became one of the most famous hotspots in New York City. Andy's work usually contained distorted brand images and celebrity faces, which was seen as a critique of his view of a culture obsessed with money and celebrity.

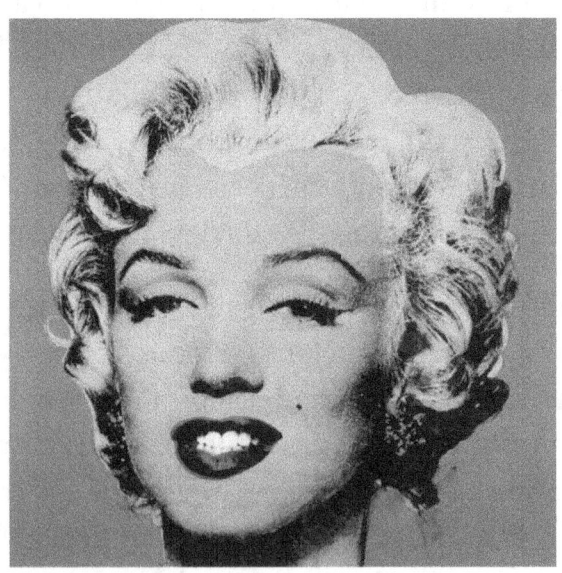

Painter Andy Worhol

## Robert Motherwell

Born in 1915 in Aberdeen, Washington, Robert Motherwell has already showed his intellectual and creative pursuits even if he was still young. He was the son of a bank chairman, and was expected to follow the footsteps of his father. He spent his education in Stanford University, Harvard University, Columbia University, and Otis Art Institute in Los Angeles. Motherwell is not only known for being artistic, he also studied philosophy and literature. It was Alfred North Whitehead, as well as the works of French poets, that inspired Motherwell to open himself to the possibilities of abstraction in writing, most especially in art.

Later on, he became the only artist in the first generation of Abstract Expressionists to utilize printmaking. Throughout his life, he spent most of his time painting, printmaking, lecturing and expanding about matters that concerned him. He died in 1991 in Provincetown, Massachusetts. His paintings are known for featuring simple shapes, bold color contrasts and a dynamic balance in brushstrokes. His works are engaged with autobiographical content and events, as well as the essential human conditions of life, death, revolution, and oppression. Some of his most famous paintings include *Ulysses, Poet,* and *Africa.*

## Bridget Riley

Bridget Riley was born in 1931 in Norwood, South London. Se was greatly influence by his father, John Fisher Riley, who was also a painter. When war broke out, she and her family had to live away to keep themselves away from danger. Her early memories of watching the changing night, color and cloud formations have had a great impact and influence on her life as an artist. Even during her early years, drawing and painting was her passion. She spent her schooling at Cheltenham Ladies College, Goldsmiths College, and Royal College of Art. Most of her paintings are black and white, and one of the most famous ones is the *Nude*.

Bridget's journey to becoming a known artist was a rough one. She encountered many difficulties along the way. She was persistent, however. That is why she continued her painting venture, as inspired by an exhibition of American Abstract Expressionist painters at the Tate Gallery. Her first paintings include black and white, with simple geometric shapes. Another known work of hers is *The Responsive Eye*. It was a hit with the public, because it raised their awareness with Op Art paintings.

**David Hockney**

David Hockney is born on the 9th of July 1937 in Bradford, Yorkshire. Before he began his painting career, he served as a hospital elderly during his early years. When he started schooling, Roger de Grey, Carel Weight, and Ceri Richards were some of his tutors.

David began dabbling in painting when he was inspired by an exhibition in London, called the Picasso exhibition. Some of his known works are *Self Portrait, Flowers, Mum, The Twenty Fourth, Jonathan Silver, Kerby, A Large Diver, Nichols*

*Canyon,* and many more. His early paintings incorporated his literary leanings, and usually used poems from Walt Whitman in his work. He is known for his homosexuality in his art as exemplified by his painting *We Two Boys Clinging Together.* He is famous for large and iconic works such as pools. He also painted interiors and exteriors of California homes. Aside from being a painter, he also devoted his time in becoming a photographer. He is also involved in lithographs, set and costume design for ballet, opera and theater.

## Mark Rothko

Mark Rothko was born on the 25th of September 1903 in Dvinsk, Russia. His full name is Marcus Rothkowitz. His father, Jacob, was a pharmacist and was married to Anna Goldin. Mark attended Yale University, studying English, European History, Freanch, mathematics, biology, economics, physics, psychology and philosophy. Before becoming an artist, he dreamt of becoming an engineer or an attorney.

Rothko is known for his attention to formal elements such as color, shape, depth, scale, balance and composition. He began his works by using myths and symbols in his paintings. Later on, he eliminated these and began working with nonobjective compositions of indeterminate shapes. *White Center* was one of his classic paintings. As time passed by, he turned to a palette of red, maroon, brown and black. He discovered a painstaking technique of overlaying colors. His paintings usually look simple, with basic shapes and colors, but all of these have symbolisms and meanings.

Mentioned above are just five of the many famous acrylic painters in the world. They have come a long and rough journey before they came to achieve their titles today. These painters and their works have contributed a lot to art. They do not only present shapes, lines, colors, and images, but most importantly, they contain meanings that are conveyed to people through their artworks. These artists serve as an inspiration for many aspiring artists, and hopefully, they inspire you too.

# Conclusion

Painting is not an easy endeavor. It requires a lot of time, effort, and passion if you want to be successful in it. More than a hobby or a career, learning to paint is a challenge that needs persistence and devotion. Truly, having knowledge about the basics of acrylic painting is necessary.

After reading about the brief history of acrylic painting, acrylic painting techniques, grades and varieties of acrylic paints, tips for beginners, and famous acrylic artists and their works, you are now prepared to take on your own painting venture.

Thank you again for downloading this book!

I hope this book was able to help you to get started, and has equipped you with enough knowledge that you would need throughout your whole painting activity. Keep this book with you as you go on, because you might need it along the way.

Enjoy painting and do not give up on your dream of becoming a great artist one day!

## Free Bonus Video: Acrylic Painting Techniques For Beginners

Included with this book is a free bonus video going over some beginner techniques that are also discussed in the book enjoy!

**Video**: https://www.youtube.com/watch?v=UazC-VIV-vg